CONSERVATION OF ENDANGERED SPECIES

SAVING THE ENDANGERED AMERICAN BALD EAGLE

THERESE SHEA

Britannica
Educational Publishing

IN ASSOCIATION WITH

ROSEN
EDUCATIONAL SERVICES

Published in 2016 by Britannica Educational Publishing (a trademark of Encyclopædia Britannica, Inc.) in association with The Rosen Publishing Group, Inc.
29 East 21st Street, New York, NY 10010

Distributed exclusively by Rosen Publishing.
To see additional Britannica Educational Publishing titles, go to rosenpublishing.com.

First Edition

Britannica Educational Publishing
J.E. Luebering: Director, Core Reference Group
Mary Rose McCudden: Editor, Britannica Student Encyclopedia

Rosen Publishing
Shalini Saxena: Editor
Nelson Sá: Art Director
Michael Moy: Designer
Cindy Reiman: Photography Manager
Sherri Jackson: Photo Researcher

Library of Congress Cataloging-in-Publication Data

Shea, Therese.
 Saving the endangered American bald eagle / Therese Shea.
      pages cm. — (Conservation of endangered species)
 Includes index.
 Audience: Grades 1 to 4.
 ISBN 978-1-68048-248-5 (library bound) — ISBN 978-1-5081-0053-9 (pbk.) — ISBN 978-1-68048-306-2
 1. Bald eagle—Juvenile literature. 2. Birds—Conservation—Juvenile literature. I. Title.
 QL696.F32S48 2015
 598.9'42—dc23
                                                                                            2015013748

Manufactured in the United States of America

Photo Credits: Cover Teri Virbickis/Shutterstock.com; back cover, p. 1, interior pages background Smileus/Shutterstock.com; p. 4 Mandel Ngan/AFP/Getty Images; p. 5 LesPalenik/Shutterstock.com; p. 6 Purestock/Thinkstock; p. 7 © Ikenberry, Donna/Animals Animals; p. 8 Gabriel Grams/Getty Images; p. 9 Sergey Uryadnikov/Shutterstock.com; p. 10 © Aitkenhead, Roger/Animals Animals; p. 11 © iStockphoto.com/Canon Bob; p. 12 predrag1/iStock/Thinkstock; p. 13 © Johnson, Johnny/Animals Animals; p. 14 Fotokostic/Shutterstock.com; p. 15 Nordic Photos/SuperStock; p. 16 Bloomberg/Getty Images; p. 17 Wallenrock/Shutterstock.com; p. 18 mscornelius/iStock/Thinkstock; p. 19 © Levin, Ted/Animals Animals; p. 20 © Tribune Content Agency LLC/Alamy; pp. 21, 27 The Washington Post/Getty Images; p. 22 The Denver Post/Getty Images; p. 23 Karen Bleier/AFP/Getty Images; p. 24 Walter Spina/iStock/Thinkstock; p. 25 lightphoto/iStock/Thinkstock; p. 26 Universal Images Group/Getty Images; p. 28 © Welling, David/Animals Animals; p. 29 Saffron Blaze/Moment/Getty Images; cover and interior pages design elements Stefanina Hill/Shutterstock.com (eagle silhouette), jurra8/Shutterstock.com (feathers)

CONTENTS

AN AMERICAN SYMBOL

Even if you have never seen a bald eagle up close, you have probably seen one on money, on a government building, or on a state or national seal. The bald eagle became the national bird of the United States in 1787. It was chosen by the Founding Fathers for several reasons. It is the only kind of eagle that lives only in North America. The bald eagle reflects the beauty of the country and is a

The bald eagle is an important symbol of the United States. It is on the presidential seal.

Compare and Contrast

Benjamin Franklin thought the turkey might be a better national bird than the bald eagle for its supposed courage. How do the birds differ? Which do you think serves as a better national symbol?

symbol of the strength and independence of the United States.

In the 1780s, there were probably hundreds of thousands of bald eagles. However, by the mid-1900s, hunters had killed many thousands. Pollution and pesticides also killed eagles. In the early 1960s, fewer than 450 pairs were left. Something had to be done to save the bald eagle.

Though bald eagles are fierce hunters themselves, they could not defend themselves from the humans who hunted them.

SPOT THE BALD EAGLE

A bald eagle can see a rabbit from about a mile (1.6 kilometers) away.

There are more than 50 species, or kinds, of eagles around the world. The bald eagle is one of two eagle species found in the United States. The bald eagle's body is dark brown with a white tail. When bald eagles become adults, the feathers on their heads turn white. These make the head look bald against the brown body even though it is not actually bald. This is how the bird got its name. The beak, eyes, and feet are yellow. Like other

Think About It

Some scientists think female eagles are larger than males so that they can hunt for different animals. Why might this be important for eagle mates?

eagles, bald eagles can see very well.

Female eagles are usually a bit larger than the males. The adult male is about 36 inches (90 centimeters) long. Its wingspan may be 6.6 feet (2 meters) wide. Females may grow to be 43 inches (108 centimeters) long and have a wingspan of 8 feet (2.5 meters).

Female bald eagles usually have larger wings, feet, and beaks than male bald eagles.

BIRDS OF PREY

All eagles are raptors, or birds of prey. This means they hunt and eat other animals. Bald eagles are sea eagles. They live along inland rivers, marshes, and large lakes. They eat mostly fish, other birds, small mammals, snakes, turtles, and crabs. An eagle that weighs about 10 pounds (4.5 kilograms) needs to eat as much as 1 pound (0.5 kilogram) of food a day. Smaller eagles need less, and larger eagles need more.

A bald eagle grabs a fish out of the Mississippi River.

Vocabulary

Talons **are the claws of an animal, especially of a bird of prey.**

Bald eagles use several hunting methods to find a meal. Their excellent eyesight lets them see prey from far away. They can swoop down from the sky to pluck fish out of the water with their **talons**. They may follow other seabirds to find fish. Bald eagles have been seen robbing seabirds, such as ospreys, of the fish they catch. They may even fight other eagles. They also eat carrion, or dead animals.

A bald eagle attacks another eagle with its talons.

HOME SWEET AERIE

Bald eagles usually mate for life. If a mate dies, the eagle chooses a new mate. The mating season differs in different parts of North America. After mating, the female lays two or three eggs in a nest.

Bald eagles build nests called aeries near water in a tall tree, on a cliff, or, very rarely, on the ground. The nest is a platform of sticks about

Bald eagles prepare their nest one to three months before they lay eggs.

Compare and Contrast

What problems do you think bald eagles in nests on the ground face that bald eagles with nests high up do not?

5 feet (1.5 meters) wide. Some older nests are almost twice this size and can weigh as much as 2 tons (1.8 metric tons). A nest in a tree could fall if the tree falls, or it can get blown down by a strong wind. If this happens, bald eagles usually rebuild the nest at or near the original site. They might also do this if they feel they are in danger.

The bald eagle builds the biggest nest of any bird in North America.

GROWING UP EAGLE

Baby eagles, or eaglets, take a bit more than a month to hatch. During that time, mother and father eagles sit on the eggs to keep them warm and out of danger. Birds such as crows and mammals such as raccoons eat unguarded eggs. Finally, the eaglets hatch with mostly brown feathers, a whitish tail, and white-lined wings.

For 2 to 3 months, both eagle parents care for their young. After about 12 weeks,

Eaglets hatch out of their eggs one at a time over several days.

Compare and Contrast

Bald eagles live as long as 30 years in the wild. Those in captivity live even longer. Why do you think this is?

the eaglets move closer to the edge of the nest, getting ready to fly. Some young eagles do not survive their first flight. Those that do stay near their parents. A young bald eagle's head turns white by the time it is four or five years old. It also begins looking for a mate around this time.

Young bald eagles like these have a mix of brown and white feathers until they are about five years old.

HATED AND HUNTED

There may have been hundreds of thousands of bald eagles when they were named the national bird of the United States. However, their numbers soon began to go down. The birds were hunted for sport. They were also hunted because people mistakenly thought the birds ate livestock. The government even offered people money to shoot them!

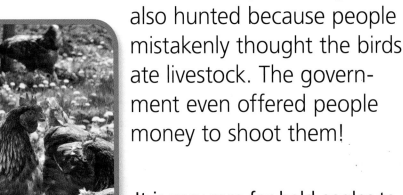

It is very rare for bald eagles to attack and kill livestock such as chickens.

Vocabulary

Extinction is the death of all members of a species.

In Alaska, bald eagles perched on fish traps and scared away salmon, an important food source for people. Alaskan hunters killed more than 100,000 bald eagles between 1917 and 1952.

Because of their shrinking numbers, the U.S. government passed the Bald Eagle Protection Act of 1940. This law made it illegal to kill bald eagles—except in Alaska. However, by the early 1960s, the number of bald eagles in the lower 48 states had dropped to fewer than 450 pairs. Bald eagles were close to extinction.

Fish might not get close to fish traps if there are bald eagles close by.

STILL DISAPPEARING

One reason for the continuing disappearance of bald eagles was the pesticide DDT. DDT was a good way to kill bugs that ate crops, and farmers began using it after World War II. However, DDT washed into the water from farms. It got into the fish in the water, and when the eagles ate the fish, the DDT got into their bodies as well. It made females lay eggs that would not hatch. It also made the eggshells

DDT was spread by planes over a wide area, not just on farms.

Vocabulary

Endangered means in danger of dying out.

thin and weak, so they broke easily. As a result, fewer eaglets were being born. In 1972, a government agency banned the use of DDT.

There were other problems as well. Scientists discovered that bald eagles were being poisoned by lead that passed into the eagles' bodies when they ate birds that had been shot with lead. Another problem for bald eagles was pollution such as oil spills. In 1978, the U.S. government declared the bald eagle an **endangered** species in most states.

The small pellets shown here are called shot. They are used in shotgun shells, seen to the right.

EAGLE AID

Government-protected land allows animal species to live without human interference.

In 1973, the U.S. government passed a law called the Endangered Species Act. When an animal is listed as endangered under the act, the animal receives special protections. It cannot be killed, captured, sold, or transported—unless one of these actions would help the species recover. The government can buy land that is known to include the species' habitat. This allows the

Compare and Contrast
The Endangered Species Act allows the U.S. government to step in when an animal is close to extinction. Can you think of other laws that protect people, animals, or plants?

government to protect the land and the animals that live on it.

Under the act, the U.S. Fish and Wildlife Service forms a recovery plan and puts it into action. It also works with other agencies or groups to make the public aware of the danger to the animal and the importance of saving it. Many steps were taken to help bald eagle numbers grow.

Scientists working for the government check the health of a bald eagle in the wild.

A scientist climbs into an aerie to place bands on eaglets so the birds can be studied.

Scientists took eggs from Florida, which had greater numbers of bald eagles, and hatched them in states where the eagle population was low. They took eggs from nests with more than two eggs and placed them with eagle pairs that did not have eggs or had eggs that did not hatch. The scientists also placed hatched eaglets in man-made nests. Scientists could not let the eaglets see them. They used camouflage as they fed the eaglets until the baby birds were ready to fly and care for themselves.

Think About It

Scientists sometimes play the role of eagle parents to help eaglets survive. Why do you think they hide themselves from the eaglets?

Scientists monitored nesting places by flying airplanes overhead so they could make sure the nests stayed safe. Building and logging could not take place in bald eagle habitats, and people were kept away. This was important because bald eagles may abandon nests if frightened.

A bald eagle is released back into the wild after being nursed back to health.

SUCCESS!

By the late 1980s, these actions had helped the wild bald eagle bounce back. In 1995, the bald eagle was named "threatened" instead of "endangered." A threatened species is one that could become endangered within several years. However, it is not as close to extinction as one that is endangered. There were about 4,500

Wildlife biologists observe the young produced by a nesting pair. They will watch them grow up.

Think About It

U.S. law also protects golden eagles, another type of eagle. However, people can get permits to remove them where they are thought to kill lambs. Do you agree with this? Why or why not?

nesting pairs in the lower 48 states. By 2000, that number increased to more than 6,300 pairs.

In 2007, the bald eagle was removed from the list of endangered and threatened species. It is still protected by the Migratory Bird Treaty Act, though not all bald eagles migrate. Also, the Bald and Golden Eagle Protection Act stops people from disturbing eagles, their nests, and their eggs without a permit. "Disturb" means to injure, bother, or cause them to change their activities.

As of 2007, the bald eagle is no longer considered an endangered species.

DON'T STOP NOW

The U.S. Fish and Wildlife Service will keep an eye on bald eagle populations for a number of years. It will survey bald eagle nests every five years. If numbers go down, the agency will figure out why and whether the eagle should be protected again under the Endangered Species Act. So far, many states report that numbers are going up.

However, bald eagle conservation is still needed. While people cannot hunt these birds,

Bald eagle families are closely watched by wildlife agencies.

Think About It

It is illegal to use lead shot when hunting waterfowl. A study showed lead shot was poisoning animals. Why do you think lead shot is not illegal for hunting other animals? Do you think it should be illegal? Why or why not?

they can still take over their habitats. Bald eagle habitats may not always be on government land that is protected.

Shorelines are popular places for people to build homes and businesses. But shorelines are nesting habitats for bald eagles. People also get lumber by cutting down trees from forests where bald eagles nest and perch.

Bald eagles sit on a building near an ocean shore.

APEX PREDATOR

You might wonder why so much trouble was taken to save the bald eagle. It is not just a U.S. symbol. Bald eagles are an important part of nature. Eagles are an apex predator. That means that they are at the top of their food chain. When fully grown, they have few or no enemies in nature. As apex predators, bald eagles keep the populations of their prey in balance. Without them, prey might become too numerous.

The hunting skills of a bald eagle help it easily pluck a fish from water.

Think About It

When pollution harms prey lower down in the food chain, apex predators are in danger, too. Why is this?

This prey might, in turn, eat too many of another species, perhaps even causing them to die out.

Also, as carrion eaters, bald eagles play an important role in cleaning up their habitats. They get rid of dead animals—by eating them!

Bald eagles eat a dead bird. Animals that eat dead animals are called scavengers.

THE OUTLOOK ON EAGLES

Bald eagles will always be an important part of their **ecosystem**. We must help bald eagles by making sure that our actions do not harm them or their way of life. Their survival means the survival of many other species. The conservation efforts that have aided bald eagles so far show that people really can make a difference in our world.

Bald eagles are beautiful birds that play a special role in nature and in the history of the United States.

Vocabulary

An ecosystem includes plants, animals, and other living and nonliving things. These things exist together in a certain place and depend on each other to live.

By changing some practices, habits, and products, the bald eagle was saved from dying out forever. Knowing why they reached such dangerously low numbers in the first place can help us stop bald eagles from becoming endangered again in the future. It may also help us understand how to protect other species that are at risk of becoming endangered or extinct. Through conservation, the world can be safe for humans and all other living things.

People were responsible for bald eagles disappearing. Now, people are keeping them safe for the future.

GLOSSARY

ABANDON To leave and never return to something.

CAMOUFLAGE A way of hiding something by covering it up or changing the way it looks.

CAPTIVITY Being held or confined so as to prevent escape.

CONSERVATION Planned management or protection of a natural resource.

HABITAT The natural place where an animal or plant lives.

HATCH To come out of an egg.

MATE To come together to make babies. Also, one of two animals that come together to make babies.

MIGRATORY Moving from one region or climate to another for feeding or breeding.

PERMIT A written statement giving permission for someone to do something.

PESTICIDE A chemical used to kill pests that cause damage to crops.

PLATFORM A raised, flat surface.

RECOVER To return to a normal state after a time of difficulty.

SHOT Small metal balls that are fired from a gun.

SURVEY To gather information about something.

WATERFOWL A bird that is found in or near water.

Books

Dolbear, Emily J. *Bald Eagles*. New York, NY: Children's Press, 2012.

Llanas, Sheila Griffin. *Bald Eagles*. Minneapolis, MN: ABDO Publishing, 2013.

McDowell, Pamela. *Bald Eagle*. New York, NY: AV2 by Weigl, 2013.

Monroe, Tyler. *The Bald Eagle*. North Mankato, MN: Capstone Press, 2014.

Nelson, Maria. *The Bald Eagle*. New York, NY: Gareth Stevens Publishing, 2015.

Rustad, Martha E. H., and Holli Conger. *Is a Bald Eagle Really Bald?* Minneapolis, MN: Millbrook Press, 2015.

Websites

Because of the changing nature of Internet links, Rosen Publishing has developed an online list of websites related to the subject of this book. This site is updated regularly. Please use this link to access the list:

http://www.rosenlinks.com/CONS/Eagle

INDEX